Chocolate Banana Pops

by **Anne Giulieri**
photography by Sylvia Kreinberg

We are going to make chocolate banana pops today.

Here is the banana.

Here is the chocolate.

Here are the rice puffs.

Here are the sprinkles.
They are red, green, blue,
and yellow!

Here are the sticks.

The banana is cut like this.

4

The sticks go here.

They go inside the banana.

The bananas
with the sticks go here.
The bananas
are going to get cold!

The chocolate goes here.
It is going to get hot!

8

The chocolate
goes onto the banana
like this.
The banana looks brown!

11

The rice puffs go onto
the chocolate banana.
They go on like this.

The sprinkles go onto
the chocolate banana.
They go on like this.

The chocolate bananas are going to get cold.

We like chocolate banana pops.
They are fun to eat!